CHICKEN POX

CHICKEN POX

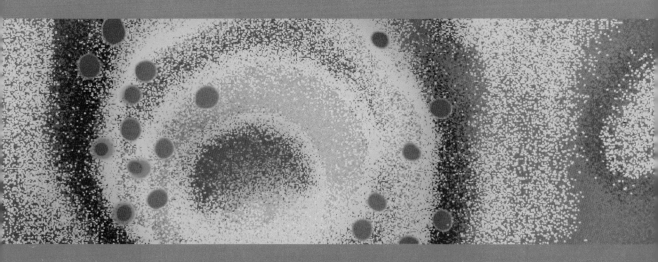

Gretchen Hoffmann

 **Marshall Cavendish**
Benchmark
New York

With thanks to Adam J. Adler, Ph.D., Associate Professor, Center for Immunotherapy of Cancer and Infectious Diseases and Department of Immunology, University of Connecticut Health Center, for his expert review of the manuscript.

Marshall Cavendish Benchmark
99 White Plains Road
Tarrytown, New York 10591-5502
www.marshallcavendish.us

This book is not intended for use as a substitute for advice, consultation, or treatment by a licensed medical practitioner. The reader is advised that no action of a medical nature should be taken without consultation with a licensed medical practitioner, including action that may seem to be indicated by the contents of this work, since individual circumstances vary and medical standards, knowledge, and practices change with time. The publisher, author, and medical consultants disclaim all liability and cannot be held responsible for any problems that may arise from use of this book.

Library of Congress Cataloging-in-Publication Data

Hoffmann, Gretchen.
Chicken pox / by Gretchen Hoffmann.
p. cm. — (Health alert)
Summary: "Provides comprehensive information on the causes, treatment, and history of chicken pox"—Provided by publisher.
Includes index.
ISBN 978-0-7614-2916-6
1. Chicken pox—Juvenile literature. I. Title.
RC125.H64 2009
616.9'14—dc22

2007031793

Cover: Varicella-Zoster viral particles, which are the cause of chicken pox
Title page: The varicella virus
Photo Research by Candlepants Incorporated
Cover Photo: © Scott Camazine / Alamy Images

The photographs in this book are used by permission and through the courtesy of: *Super Stock*: SuperStock, Inc. 3, 12; age fotostock, 22, 24. *PhotoTakeUSA.com*: Dennis Kunkel, 5, 18; Carol Donner, 20; Nucleus Medical Art, Inc, 21; Bart's Medical Library, 29. *Alamy Images*: © David White, 7; © Phototake Inc., 9; © Bubbles Photolibrary, 16, 54; © Picture Partners, 50; © Medical-on-Line, 51; © Craig Holmes, 52. *Getty Images*: William Radcliffe, 10; SIU, 30; Stuart McClymont, 45; George Musil, 28. *Photo Researchers Inc.*: Dr P. Marazzi, 13, 40; Jean-Loup Charmet, 34. *Corbis*: Lester V. Bergman, 14; Bettmann, 32, 47; CDC/PHIL, 35; Luis Alonso/EFE, 37; Reuters, 38; Holger Winkler/zefa, 26. *Shutterstock*: 43.

Editor: Joy Bean
Publisher: Michelle Bisson
Art Director: Anahid Hamparian

Printed in Malaysia
6 5 4 3 2 1

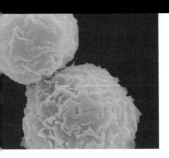

CONTENTS

WHAT IS IT LIKE TO HAVE CHICKEN POX?

Kathy sat in the waiting room of her doctor's office with her mother and her younger brother, Chris. She did not feel sick, and Chris was not sick either, so when her mother told her this morning that they were going to the doctor's office, she wondered why. Her mother explained that Kathy and Chris were both going to get a special treatment called a **vaccine** that would prevent them from getting an infection called chicken pox.

Chris, who was almost five years old, thought that chicken pox was a funny-sounding name and started making clucking noises and flapping his arms like a chicken. Kathy and her mom laughed. "No, no," said their mother. "Chicken pox does not turn you into a chicken, silly!" She explained that chicken pox is a **contagious**, itchy rash, and that when infected, children must stay home from school for at least a week so as not to make other people sick.

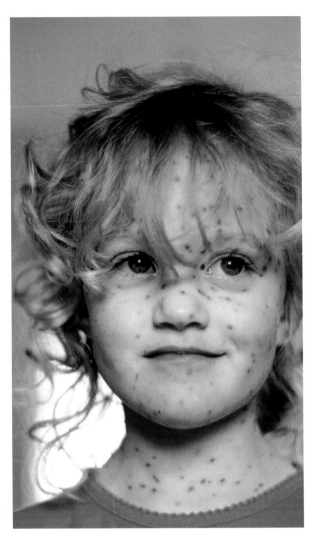

Chicken pox can look like insect bites.

Kathy, who was soon to be ten years old, had heard about chicken pox. A few years ago, some of her classmates had chicken pox and stayed home from school for a while, but she did not catch it from them. When they returned to class they still had some of the crusty little bumps on their faces, necks, and arms. One boy lifted up his shirt and showed the rest of the class how the bumps had covered his entire belly! They talked about what it had been like having itchy insect bites all over their bodies. One girl said that it had been really difficult not to scratch the bumps, and that she even wore gloves to help keep herself from picking at the scabs. Another boy said that his spots were just as painful as they were itchy and that he had a hard time getting comfortable when he was going to sleep or just lying on the sofa to read or to watch a movie.

Kathy thought that staying home from school for a week actually sounded like a fun idea. What was the big deal about a few itchy spots anyway? Kathy's mom told her what it was like when she was a little girl. "Everyone got chicken pox when I was a kid. Everyone who lived on my street and played games together had them at the same time. It was really hard not to scratch the bumps because they were so itchy. I had a fever and had to stay in bed for a few days to rest. But I was lucky because other kids had it much worse. A lot of my friends got very sick and had a terrible rash that was very painful and itchy."

People today who do not get vaccinated with the chicken pox vaccine are more likely to catch chicken pox from someone else because it is a highly contagious illness, which means it is very easily passed from person to person. The chicken pox vaccine was not available when Kathy's mother was young. All of her mother's classmates and neighborhood friends had chicken pox at the same time because they were not protected by the vaccine, but Kathy did not get sick when her own friends were infected because she had already received the first dose of the vaccine.

Kathy had been given one dose of the chicken pox vaccine as a baby after her first birthday. The vaccine was a shot that helped protect Kathy from the illness by introducing her body's

immune system to a very weak form of the chicken pox **virus**. That way her body was able to destroy the virus and would help prevent her from getting sick in the future. Kathy's brother Chris had also already had one shot when he was a baby, but their doctor had recommended that they come back to the office for a second dose. "And that is the reason we came to the doctor's office today," her mother said. "You and Chris both need a second injection of the vaccine to protect you from getting chicken pox completely."

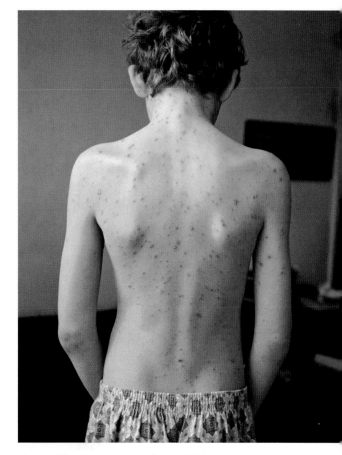

The red bumps that are from chicken pox are itchy and can appear anywhere on the body.

When Chris heard that he was about to get a shot, he started to get nervous. But in the examination room, he only felt a little sting and a pinch when the nurse gave him his shot. Kathy hardly felt her vaccine shot at all, and now she and her brother would both be protected against the itchy, contagious infection known as chicken pox.

[2]

WHAT IS CHICKEN POX?

Chicken pox, also called varicella, is a highly contagious illness. That means when someone is infected with chicken pox, it is very likely that people he or she is living with or going to school with will also become infected if they are not

The chicken pox virus is so contagious, it can be spread through the air by a person sneezing.

already protected from the illness. It can be spread from person to person through the air or by contact with the bumps of the chicken pox rash itself. When an infected person sneezes or coughs, tiny droplets of water loaded with the chicken pox virus shoot out of the mouth and nose. The sneeze can carry the virus several feet through the air. It might land on someone directly, or be breathed in by someone nearby, and that person will then be at risk for developing chicken pox.

Although the name might mislead you into thinking this illness has something to do with chickens or birds, it does not. Humans are the only living creatures that can get chicken pox. Chicken pox infects males and females equally. It occurs worldwide and individuals of all races are **susceptible** to the illness.

Chicken pox is caused by the varicella-zoster virus. A virus is a tiny organism that can cause infection. Since the late 1800s, scientists have known that **microbes**, such as bacteria and viruses, cause infections. Viruses are much smaller than bacteria and can be shaped like a rod, sphere, or have many sides like a crystal. They cannot survive for long outside a living creature, called a **host**, because viruses depend on the host to produce all of the materials it needs to survive and reproduce. The virus itself is made only of **DNA** or **RNA** wrapped in a coating of **protein**. The DNA or RNA contains **genes**, which

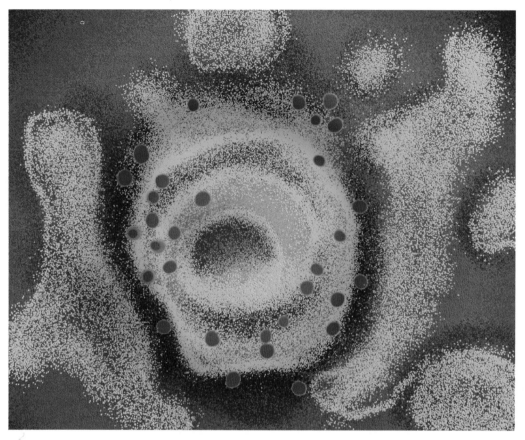

The varicella-zoster virus, seen here, is what causes chicken pox.

are the instructions a cell uses to carry out a specific job and produce different proteins. Because viruses consist only of this genetic material and not of cells, they rely on the host and the host's cells to do all the work. It is as if the virus has a recipe, but no ingredients or equipment to make the end product. That is why it uses the supplies and equipment of the host's cells to reproduce and survive.

A person infected with chicken pox usually gets the virus through the cells lining the inside of the nose, mouth, or eyes. Then the virus gets to work directing the infected cells to start making many copies of itself. This process of copying the virus is called **replicating**. After a few days, the copies of the varicella virus travel to the liver, spleen, and other organs and continue to replicate.

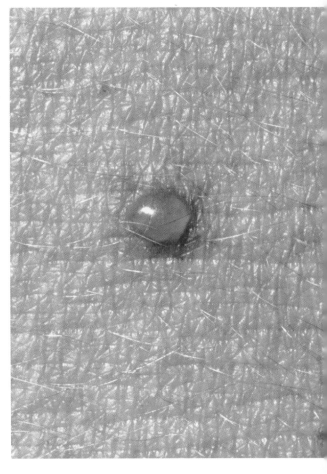

Approximately fourteen days later, the viral infection reaches the skin. Overall, it takes between ten and twenty-one days following exposure to the virus before the **symptoms** begin to appear. So by the time symptoms start to show, the infected person has already had the virus for a few weeks.

SYMPTOMS

An itchy, red rash is the main symptom of chicken pox. The itchy spots, also called lesions or blisters, can take different shapes and forms. Depending on how recently the lesion appeared on

A chicken pox lesion, before it has been popped.

the skin, it might look solid and resemble an insect bite or be filled with fluid and look almost like a water droplet. The spots quickly fill with a clear fluid, rupture (break open and release the liquid inside), and then turn crusty. The blisters can pop open on their own, but they usually break when they are scratched or rub against something like clothing or bed sheets. New blisters continue to appear as the older ones become crusted over, so a person can have blisters in different stages of healing on the same part of the body.

The number of spots that develop is different for each person, but on average a person will develop 250–500 lesions.

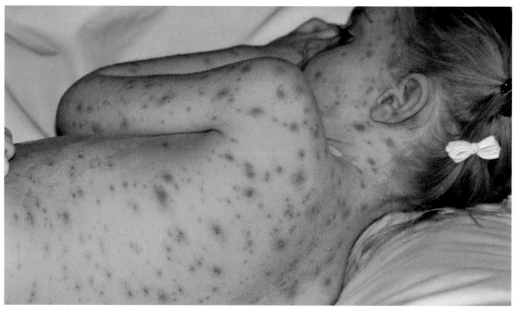

The number of chicken pox spots a person develops varies, but some people can have as many as five hundred on their body.

The bumps are usually round or oval shaped. Most are small, about the size of an eraser on a pencil, but can be twice that size. The blisters can form anywhere on the body, but are most commonly on the chest and abdomen. Blisters can also develop on the arms, legs, face, and on the scalp, which is the skin under the hair on your head. Lesions can sometimes occur inside the mouth, throat, and on the tongue, which can make it painful to eat and drink, and blisters can even develop in the eyes. The bumps form a scab a few days after appearing. Scabs are an important part of the healing process. The scab covering the blister helps keep out bacteria while the skin underneath heals. Picking off the scab can lead to infection or to a scar. Chicken pox scars are called pockmarks. The crusts completely fall off within one or two weeks after they first appeared. The chicken pox virus is

The word pox is actually another way to spell the word *pocks*, which can mean swollen, pus-filled sores. There are a number of other diseases known as poxes, including smallpox and cowpox. Why did this disease become known as chicken pox if it does not come from or affect chickens? It might be a variation on the word *gican*, which in Old English meant "to itch," or it might be because the blisters resemble the beans known as chickpeas. No one knows for sure.

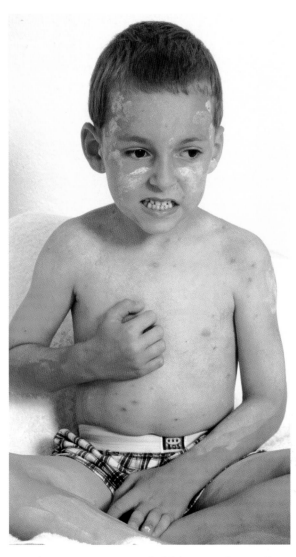

The worst symptom of chicken pox is usually the itchiness.

contagious for one to two days before the rash appears and until all the blisters have formed scabs.

Usually the worst symptom of chicken pox is feeling itchy all over. The irritation can range from moderately annoying to severely uncomfortable. The itchiness tends to get better as the blisters scab over, however. And even though the rash may be very itchy and uncomfortable, people with chicken pox must try to stop themselves from scratching the sores and scabs because scratching can lead to infections and cause permanent scars on the skin.

Some people experience a mild cough and runny nose during the first two days of illness before the rash appears. People who have chicken pox often also have a headache, and they generally feel tired or sore as well as very itchy. They may also experience a sore throat or loss of appetite.

Chicken pox is most common in children younger than fifteen years old and is usually mild with no lasting consequences. But it can be serious, and certain groups of people are more likely to have a more severe case of chicken pox and are at risk for more serious **complications**. Young children usually have milder symptoms and fewer blisters than infants, older children, or adults. People with weakened immune systems due to other illnesses or medications they are taking are also at higher risk for a more severe case of chicken pox. Chicken pox also tends to be worse in children who have other skin problems.

DEVELOPING IMMUNITY

People usually get chicken pox just once in their lifetime. That is because, once infected, the body's immune system develops a special protection against the infection. This protection is called **immunity**. The immune system is made up of a network of organs, cells, and proteins that work together to identify and defend against harmful invaders known as **pathogens**. Viruses, certain bacteria, and other **microorganisms** that do not belong in the body are all pathogens. These foreign invaders are recognized by some of the body's most important cells in the immune system—the white blood cells. These cells have the job of

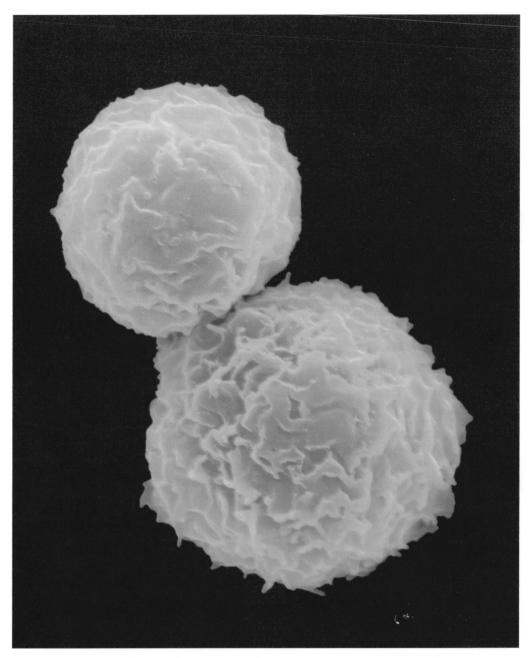

The body's T-cells (top) and B-cells (bottom) help protect the body from infection.

patrolling the body and recognizing when something is unfamiliar and potentially harmful. Some white blood cells are even more specialized. These cells, the T-cells and B-cells, are called **lymphocytes**. Each of these cell types has a unique role in the immune system.

The job of T-cells is to coordinate the immune system's attack on pathogens. T-cells give instructions to other cells on where to go and when to attack. They communicate by using **molecules** that pass messages between cells so that the entire network is working toward the same goal. T-cells also help organize the actions of B-cells.

The job of B-cells is to produce protective molecules called **antibodies**. Antibodies are made specifically to attack a certain threat. When a B-cell meets up with a pathogen for the first time, the lymphocyte recognizes that the invader does not belong in the body because it has certain molecules on its surface that do not match the rest of the body's cells and proteins. These molecules are called **antigens**. The B-cell then produces an antibody to fight against that specific antigen. The antibodies attach to the virus or bacteria and prepare the immune system to destroy that pathogen. Each B-cell can recognize only one antigen and produce one type of antibody. Therefore, the body produces millions of B-cells that travel through the body and are ready to recognize and attack many different types of antigens.

An antibody created by a B-cell has attached itself to a virus to let the body know there is an invader that does not belong.

There are, however, some T-cells and B-cells, called memory cells, that can remember a certain antigen for a very long time. So, when the same infection happens again, those cells are able to quickly recognize it and start actively fighting it. T-cells direct the attack, and B-cells start producing an army of copies of the correct antibody against that antigen.

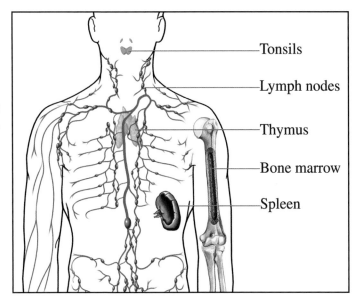

Tonsils

Lymph nodes

Thymus

Bone marrow

Spleen

The thymus is an important part of the immune system. It tells the body which substances belong in the body and which do not.

These white blood cells are produced by the **bone marrow** and the **thymus**, which are two important parts of the immune system. Bone marrow is the spongy material that fills the inside of bones. It produces B-cells along with other blood cells including red blood cells that carry oxygen and platelets that help blood clot. The thymus is located in the upper chest. It is in the thymus that T-cells are produced and learn to differentiate the substances that belong in the body from those that do not.

People can develop immunity in several ways. One way is by being exposed to a pathogen through everyday life, as when someone sneezes and others breathe in the germs floating in the air. When the immune system develops antibodies against an invader this way, it is called naturally acquired immunity. Naturally acquired immunity also occurs when babies receive antibodies from their mothers' immune systems before being born and through drinking breast milk after birth.

Another way people can develop immunity is through a type of protection known as artificial immunity. It has the same result as naturally acquired immunity—the body creates antibodies to fight a certain illness—but a person does not have to get sick before becoming immune because the source of the antigen is provided deliberately by giving a vaccine. Vaccination is a safe way to expose the body to a small amount of a pathogen in order to trigger the immune system to fight that specific infection. Usually vaccines are given as an injection using a needle. Some newer vaccines can be inhaled by breathing in a mist through the nose. Regardless of how the vaccine is given, all vaccines contain a pathogen that has been altered in some way so that it cannot make a person sick but can

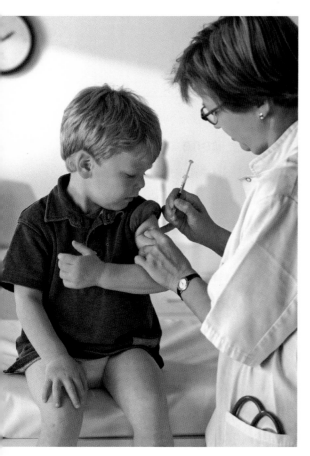

Vaccines contain a weakened form of a virus.

still trigger the immune system to destroy the foreign invader. The pathogen in the vaccine might be very weak or killed, or sometimes the vaccine contains only a small part of the pathogen. The immune system detects the pathogen in the vaccine and triggers B-cells to produce antibodies against it. These B-cells will remember the specific enemy introduced by the vaccine and will be ready to fight by producing effective antibodies if the real pathogen attacks later on.

WHO GETS CHICKEN POX?

Before the vaccine was available, chicken pox was a very common childhood illness because it is so contagious. Most children had already had chicken pox by the time they were teenagers. In fact, most cases of chicken pox appeared in people younger than fifteen years old. However, older teenagers and adults can still get chicken pox if they never had it as a young child. Having the chicken pox during early childhood is actually better than having it later in life, because younger children often have milder symptoms and fewer bumps than older children or adults. Young children are also less likely to develop complications than very young babies or adults. That is why in the past, some parents tried to get their children infected with chicken pox when other siblings, classmates, or friends had the infection. They did this because by getting the

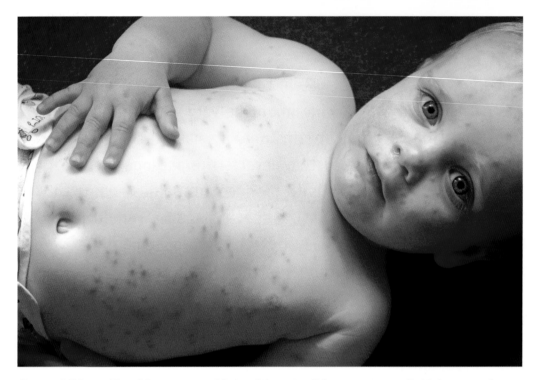

Young children, like this one year old, tend to get milder symptoms of chicken pox than those who are older.

infection early in life, their children would be protected from getting chicken pox later when it could be much worse. Doctors do not encourage parents to do this today. Instead, they encourage parents to have their children immunized against the disease with the chicken pox vaccine.

COMPLICATIONS

Chicken pox is normally a mild disease. The rash and other symptoms of chicken pox usually resolve in a few weeks, leading to a full recovery. But just like other **infectious** diseases, chicken pox can be serious and can lead to complications. The most common complication of chicken pox is a bacterial infection of the skin. If the surrounding skin or the bumps themselves become very red, warm, or tender, this may indicated a secondary bacterial skin infection that needs additional treatment. A person should see a doctor if the rash spreads to one or both eyes to make sure that the blisters will not damage eyesight. Dizziness, disorientation, rapid heartbeat, shortness of breath, loss of muscle coordination, worsening cough, vomiting, stiff neck, or a fever higher than 103 degrees Fahrenheit (39.4 degrees Celsius) are also reasons to see a doctor for further examination.

Serious complications of chicken pox are not common, but may include severe skin infection, scars, pneumonia, brain damage, or death. Chicken pox may lead to an **inflammation** of the brain called encephalitis, which can be very serious. Pneumonia, although rare, is another serious complication. People who smoke and those with lung infections are at greatest risk of developing this complication.

Some people are at higher risk for developing complications than others. Newborns and infants whose mothers never had chicken pox or the vaccine are at higher risk, as are teenagers and adults whose mothers were not immune. People whose immune systems are impaired by another disease or condition, or who are taking steroid medications are also at higher risk for

Pregnant women should be careful to not get chicken pox because the virus can cause birth defects in the unborn child.

complications. In addition, it is very dangerous for a pregnant woman to get chicken pox, especially during the first twenty weeks of pregnancy or in the few weeks before the baby is born. Being infected with varicella early in a pregnancy increases the chance of the child having serious birth defects, such as shortened arms and legs, scarring, cataracts (a cloudy area in the lens of the eye that prohibits sight), small head size, abnormal brain development, and mental defects. If a pregnant woman is infected with chicken pox within a few days of giving birth, the baby may develop a severe case of it and may need immediate medical attention.

REACTIVATION OF THE VARICELLA-ZOSTER VIRUS

Although it is very unlikely for someone to be reinfected with a second case of chicken pox, the varicella-zoster virus can cause another infection much later in life. The virus never really leaves the body completely after the initial chicken pox infection. After the chicken pox scabs have healed, the person recovers, but the virus is not dead. It is inactive, but still alive in the body. This is known as a latent infection because the virus remains silent and hidden and does not cause symptoms. A healthy immune system keeps the virus inactive and prevents it from causing any symptoms. However, sometimes as people age or if their immune systems are weakened, their bodies are unable to keep the varicella-zoster virus in this inactive state. It is as if the virus suddenly wakes up after being asleep for many years. Scientists do not know exactly what happens to reactivate the virus, but when it does, the person will suffer from a new infection caused by the same virus. This infection, called herpes zoster, is also known as shingles.

A person with a shingles rash can pass the virus to someone who has never had chicken pox, but that person will develop chicken pox, not shingles. It does not work the other way around: A person with chicken pox cannot give someone shingles. This is because shingles comes from the virus hiding inside the person's body, not from an outside source. A person can develop shingles only if he or she has had the chicken pox in the past.

While the varicella-zoster virus is in hiding, it stays inside a person's nerve cells. These cells are usually sensory nerves that

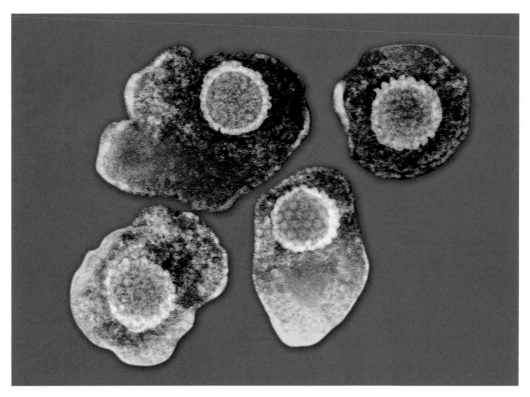

The varicella-zoster virus, from the herpes family, causes chicken pox as well as shingles.

are in the spine. They send signals of temperature, pain, pressure, and other sensations from different parts of the body to the brain. When the varicella-zoster virus reactivates, the virus moves back down the long nerve fibers that extend to the skin.

Because shingles affects the nervous system, the rash is often more painful than the itchy bumps of chicken pox. It tends to trace the path of the nerves inside the body as a visible rash on the skin. The rash begins with reddish bumps that turn into blisters. The blisters usually cluster in one

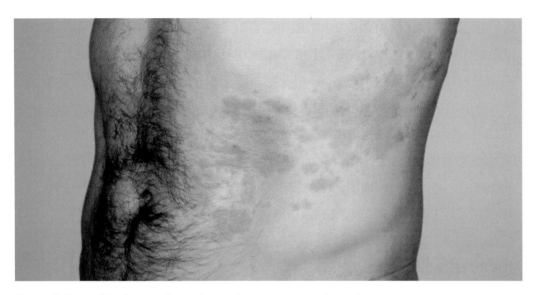

The rash from shingles tends to cluster in one area, such as the torso.

specific area, rather than scatter all over the body as with chicken pox. The **torso** and face are the areas most likely to be affected. Like chicken pox, shingles can affect the eyes, causing swollen eyelids, redness, and pain. This should be monitored closely because shingles blisters in the eyes can cause scars that may permanently affect vision.

Shingles pain can be mild or intense. It can feel like burning, stabbing, itching, or aching. Some people feel pain from the gentlest touch or even from air blowing across the sensitive area. Even though the rash gets better or goes away in a few weeks, the pain may last longer. In most people, the pain goes away within a few weeks, but it can sometimes continue long after the rash has disappeared. This type of pain is called postherpetic neuralgia. About one fifth of people who get shingles suffer from this type of pain, which can last for years after the rash has healed. The pain can make it difficult to do normal daily activities and may also make people feel depressed. Regular pain medications that can be bought without a prescription may not be able to stop the pain resulting from shingles. Patients may need to work with a doctor to try stronger treatments to help ease their pain. Also, damage can occur to the eyes or other organs if they are affected.

It is estimated that one million people are affected by herpes zoster in the United States each year. The risk of getting

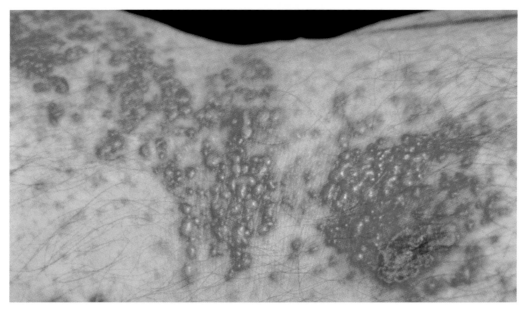

An up-close look at the blisters from shingles is seen here.

shingles increases with age. For example, people in their seventies and eighties are much more likely to get shingles than are people in their fifties and sixties. More than half of people who live to be eighty-five years old will have herpes zoster at some point in their lives. Elderly people are also more likely than young people to have a severe case of the shingles and are more likely to be hospitalized because of the infection. People in their thirties and forties can also develop shingles, but it is less likely to cause serious or lasting pain.

For a long time doctors could do nothing to prevent herpes zoster. They could only give patients drugs in order to speed the healing of the rash and ease the pain once the infection developed. Today there is a vaccine available that helps prevent shingles. It is similar to the vaccine that is now available to prevent the original infection that causes chicken pox. People age sixty or older can get this new vaccine that helps the body's immune system keep up the defense against the varicella-zoster virus. It boosts the body's immunity, which may be getting weaker with age. People who are vaccinated are less likely to develop shingles, but if they do, they are more likely to have a milder case.

3

THE HISTORY OF CHICKEN POX

Until the 1900s, chicken pox was sometimes confused with smallpox, which is a much more serious illness. They both share the symptom of a rash with red sores, yet chicken pox is different from smallpox in several important ways. Smallpox sores are most common on the face, arms, and legs, while chicken pox sores are most common on the back, chest, and abdomen. Smallpox lesions are also much deeper and are more likely to leave a scar than chicken pox lesions. Also, chicken pox blisters can be at all different

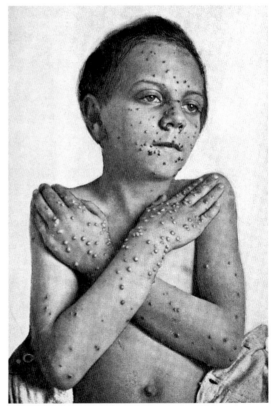

A smallpox vaccine had not been created yet when this boy got the virus in 1915.

stages in the same area of the body at one time, while all of the smallpox lesions in a given area are at the same stage.

In 1875, a scientist discovered that chicken pox was caused by an infectious agent. The researcher, Rudolf Steiner, took fluid from the chicken pox blisters of an infected person and rubbed it on the skin of healthy volunteers. They, too, developed the itchy, bumpy rash. Similar observations were made by a researcher named James von Bokay, who wrote about chicken pox infections in individuals who had close contact with others suffering from shingles. This proved that chicken pox was an infectious disease that could be passed along by contact between people. Research done from the 1920s through the 1950s proved that chicken pox (varicella) and shingles (zoster) were both caused by the same virus, the varicella-zoster virus. A scientist named Thomas Weller recovered the varicella-zoster virus from the fluid of both chicken pox and shingles blisters and grew the virus in a laboratory. By 1958, Weller and his colleagues had proven without question that the two infections were caused by the varicella-zoster virus.

After scientists discovered the viral cause of chicken pox, they used knowledge gained from other diseases that had been successfully treated and started working on creating a vaccine to prevent infection with the varicella-zoster virus. The history of vaccines began more than two hundred years ago, when Dr. Edward Jenner laid the foundation with his work on smallpox.

Dr. Edward Jenner, seen here, helped create the first vaccines.

He discovered that vaccines using the relatively harmless cowpox virus could protect people from getting infected with the deadly smallpox virus. While living in the United Kingdom, Dr. Jenner noticed that some young women seemed protected from smallpox if they had already been infected by the much less dangerous virus that caused cowpox. Cowpox is caused by the vaccinia virus and normally affects the udders of cows, but can be spread to humans. It causes a red skin rash and abnormally enlarged lymph nodes—symptoms much like the more serious smallpox virus. In 1796, he conducted a very important experiment. First, Dr. Jenner took some fluid and material from a cowpox sore. Then he scratched the arm of an eight-year-old boy with the sample, infecting him with cowpox. He then repeated the experiment, but added a small amount of material from a smallpox sore and waited to see what happened. As he predicted, the boy did not develop the deadly smallpox infection. The cowpox infection had immunized the boy against smallpox and protected him from getting sick. Dr. Jenner had created and used the first vaccine. In fact, the words *vaccine* and *vaccination* come from Dr. Jenner's initial experiments with cowpox, as the Latin word *vacca* means of or from cows. By around 1800, cowpox vaccinations were commonly given because they caused fewer side effects and deaths than did smallpox. About a century after Dr. Jenner's pioneering work, Dr. Louis Pasteur showed that he could pre-vent rabies by infecting humans with

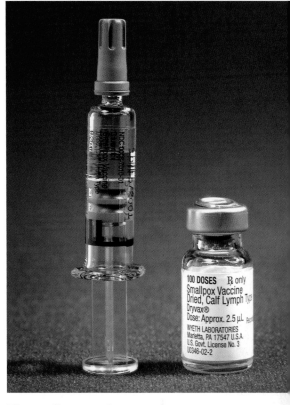

The smallpox vaccine.

weakened germs. In the mid 1900s, Dr. Jonas Salk developed the inactivated polio vaccine that has saved millions of chil-dren from the physical disability of polio.

Dr. Jenner's discovery paved the way for the development of vaccines for other diseases as well, and there are now many infectious diseases that can be prevented by vaccination. Smallpox was declared officially eliminated from the world

Smallpox Vaccine

Smallpox is a highly contagious disease caused by the variola virus. Some experts say that over the centuries it has killed more people than all other infectious diseases combined. Smallpox was described thousands of years ago in ancient Egyptian and Chinese writings. Although it has killed hundreds of millions of people throughout history, worldwide **immunization** finally stopped the spread of this disease. Thanks to the success of the smallpox vaccine, the last case was reported in 1977, and today children no longer receive the smallpox vaccine as a routine immunization. Smallpox was said to be wiped out worldwide by 1980, and no cases of naturally occurring smallpox have happened since.

The initial signs and symptoms of smallpox are fever, fatigue, and headache—much like the flu. Later, severe blisters appear on the skin that can leave deep scars. There is no effective treatment for smallpox and no known cure once symptoms develop. The majority of people with smallpox recover, but death may occur in up to 30 percent of cases. Those who do recover are often left with disfiguring scars.

The vaccinia virus, which is closely related to the variola virus that causes smallpox, was used to make a smallpox vaccine. The vaccinia virus is also closely related to the virus that causes cowpox that Dr. Jenner used in his experiments. Most people experience normal, typically mild reactions to the vaccine, which go away without treatment. The vaccine often causes a low fever, and swollen glands in the armpits, as well as red skin at the vaccination site. Because the currently available smallpox vaccine can also have severe and sometimes deadly side effects, researchers are pursuing the development of new, safer vaccines against smallpox.

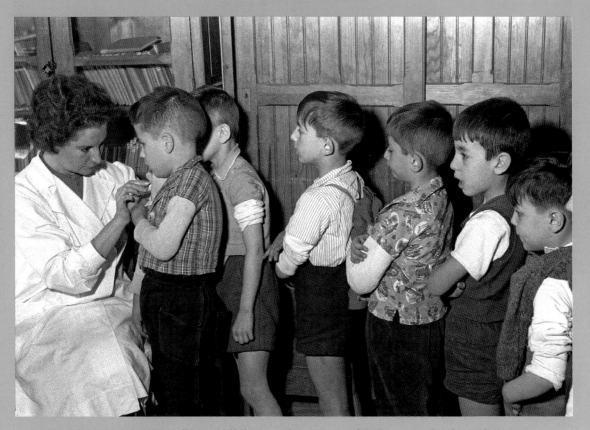

To stop the spread of smallpox, children used to get vaccinations at school, as these children were in 1961.

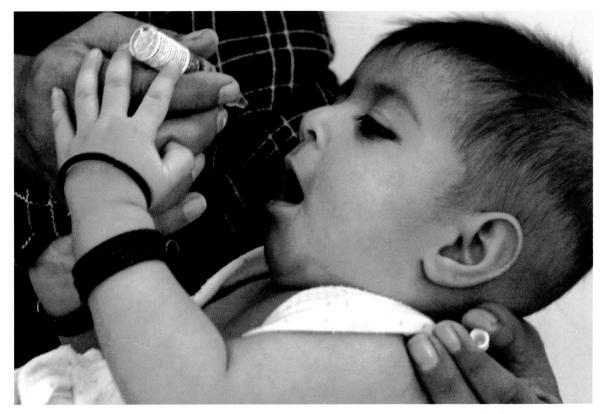

The polio vaccine can be taken in liquid form by mouth, so that no needles are involved.

several decades ago, and not a single case of polio, another previously highly contagious disease, has been reported in the United States since 1979.

The chicken pox vaccine was developed in Japan in the 1970s. In 1974, a researcher named Michiaki Takahashi and his colleagues developed a way to weaken the varicella virus enough so that it was safe to use in a vaccine. It did not cause an active infection but was still able to be recognized by the immune system as a pathogen. Starting in the 1980s, the vaccine was tested in **clinical trials** to make sure that it was safe to use in humans and was effective in preventing the infection. The vaccine became available in the United States in 1995.

Before the chicken pox vaccine was available, it is estimated that four million people got chicken pox each year. But today, the number of people who get chicken pox each year is very low. It is estimated that the number of chicken pox cases each year has dropped to less than 25 percent of the yearly totals before the vaccine became available. The number may actually be as low as 10 percent, compared with pre-vaccine totals.

Infectious Diseases That Can Be Prevented by Vaccine

Chicken pox
Cholera
Diphtheria
Hepatitis A and B
Influenza
Measles
Mumps
Pertussis (whooping cough)
Polio
Rabies
Rubella
Shingles
Smallpox
Tetanus
Typhoid fever
Yellow fever

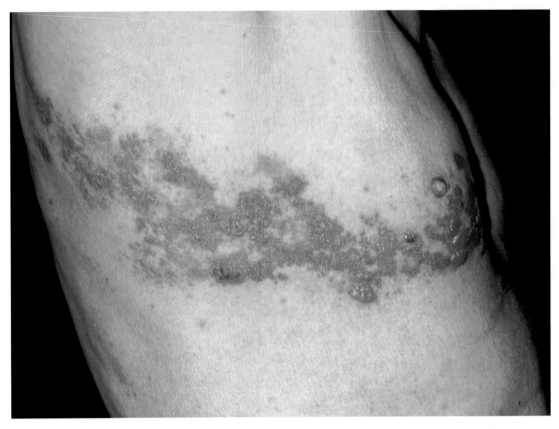

Older people tend to get the shingles virus, like this 90-year-old man, who is showing symptoms on his chest.

Additionally, approximately 11,000 people were hospitalized and about 100 people died each year from chicken pox before the vaccine was available. Today, this is not a concern and very few people die or are hospitalized because of chicken pox. In fact, the number of people who have had to go to the hospital or have died from varicella has declined substantially by more than 90 percent since the vaccine was introduced.

In 2006, a vaccine to reduce the risk of shingles was approved for use in the United States. This vaccine can be given to people age sixty and older who have had chicken pox. Researchers have found that giving older adults the vaccine reduced the expected number of cases of shingles by half. And in people who still got shingles despite immunization, it was much less severe and had fewer complications. The shingles vaccine, however, works only to try to prevent the illness, and is not a treatment for those who already have shingles or the lasting pain associated with it.

4

PREVENTING, DIAGNOSING, AND TREATING CHICKEN POX

The best way to prevent getting chicken pox is to be vaccinated. The chicken pox vaccine is recommended for all **susceptible** children and adults. The vaccine is actually a small dose of a highly weakened varicella-zoster virus. The virus is alive, but it is so weak that it cannot cause a full infection. The vaccine is given as an injection that triggers the immune system to fight and produce antibodies against the virus. Should the real virus attack later on, the immune system will be ready to produce the right antibodies to fight against the virus and prevent chicken pox from developing at all, or make the illness much less serious should it develop.

Some vaccines last a lifetime, while others must be administered multiple times. The T-cells and B-cells of the immune system will remember the varicella virus from the first vaccine shot for a long time. In fact, receiving one dose of the varicella

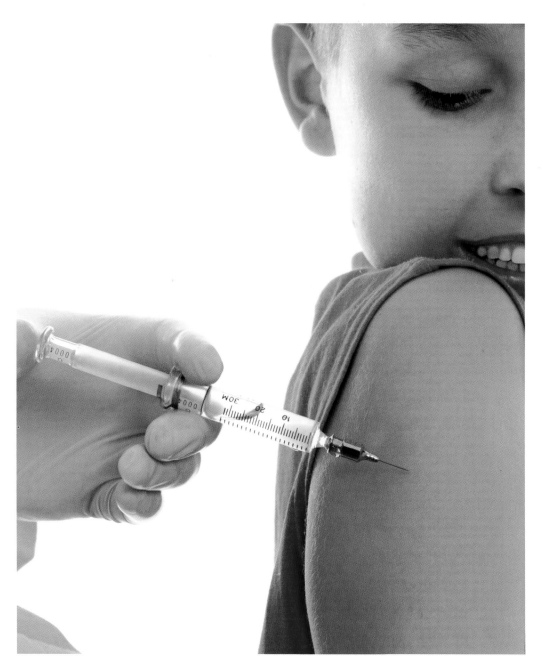

The chicken pox vaccine is recommended for all susceptible children.

vaccine has proven to be approximately 85 percent effective at preventing chicken pox. It is also able to prevent severe chicken pox in more than 95 percent of vaccinated people. However, a person's immunity can be even stronger if a second dose of the vaccine is given later in life. That is why doctors now recommend that everyone receive the varicella vaccine twice. This is a change from the original recommendations created when the vaccine was first available. At that time, doctors only gave one dose of the vaccine during a person's entire lifetime, and it was usually given after a child turned one year old. Now, it is recommended to receive the first dose between ages twelve and fifteen months and the second dose later when the child is between four and six years old. If a child older than six years has only received one dose, doctors now recommend giving a second catch-up dose. Also, adolescents and adults can still be vaccinated if they missed the first dose as a baby. People who have never had chicken pox or have never been vaccinated against chicken pox and are thirteen years old or older can receive two doses of the vaccine. The doctor will give one injection and then wait four to eight weeks to give the second.

The chicken pox vaccine is also available in combination with another vaccine that children receive early in life, called the MMR vaccine. This shot protects against three other illnesses: measles (M), mumps (M), and rubella (R). The

Having the chicken pox may mean having a fever and a general feeling of being unwell.

new vaccine is now called MMRV, adding the V for varicella.

Side effects from the chicken pox vaccine are very mild and usually not serious. The risk of getting the infection is much greater than the risk of getting side effects after being vaccinated. The chance of having a serious complication is extremely small, but the vaccine can cause a few mild problems. Some people may have a mild allergic reaction to the shot.

MMR Vaccine

....

The MMR vaccine combines vaccines for measles, mumps, and rubella into one injection. The combination vaccine has been available since 1971, and each separate vaccine was available for several years before that. Before the vaccine, all three of these viral illnesses were common childhood infections. Measles causes a rash all over the body, fever, runny nose, and cough. It is spread through the air by coughing and sneezing. Before the vaccine, nearly all Americans got measles by the time they were teenagers, and it affected nearly a half-million people in the United States every year. Currently, only about fifty people get measles in the United States each year, and most of these cases are in people who travel outside the country where measles is still a common problem. Mumps is also spread through the air. It causes an inflammation in the glands that produce saliva in the cheeks and jaw and causes the face to swell. Before the vaccine, about 200,000 cases were reported each year in the United States. Now mumps is very uncommon, with about two hundred cases reported yearly. Rubella resembles measles and is especially dangerous to unborn babies when a mother is infected during pregnancy. Infection can result in miscarriage or multiple birth defects. From 1964 to 1965 there was an outbreak of rubella that affected about 12.5 million people, but now there are fewer than twenty cases of rubella currently reported each year in the United States.

These siblings, who caught the mumps virus in 1948, had to stay inside because mumps is spread through the air. The mumps, which causes the face to swell, is very uncommon nowadays.

The area around the injection site may feel sore or appear slightly swollen. Some people may develop a fever or a mild rash after getting the vaccine. These mild effects generally do not last long and usually go away without treatment. However, a doctor should be consulted right away if symptoms of a more serious reaction to the vaccine appear. These signs— including high fever, sudden changes in behavior, difficulty breathing, wheezing, hives, paleness, weakness, fast heartbeat, and dizziness—may indicate a severe allergic reaction that requires immediate medical attention.

Some people should not get the chicken pox vaccine or may need to wait to get it. For example, if someone has had a serious allergic reaction to gelatin or the antibiotic neomycin, he or she should not get the chicken pox vaccine. And people whose immune systems may be weakened due to disease or medication also should not receive the varicella vaccine. This includes people with leukemia or other cancers, and people taking high doses of steroid medications. Also, women who are pregnant or trying to get pregnant should not get the vaccine. People who are moderately or severely sick with another illness at the time they are scheduled to receive the vaccine should wait until they recover because the vaccine could make them even sicker if their immune system is already weakened. Infants should not be given this vaccine, so doctors wait until after a child's first birthday to vaccinate them against chicken pox.

Sometimes a person can have a very mild case of chicken pox even though he or she received the vaccine. Doctors call this a "breakthrough infection." Compared with people who have not been vaccinated and who get chicken pox, incidents of breakthrough infections are usually much milder cases. Vaccinated people who show signs of infection are ill for a shorter amount of time and are less likely to have a fever. They usually have less than fifty lesions, which is considerably less than a typical case of chicken pox.

OTHER WAYS TO PREVENT CHICKEN POX

There are other simple steps that can be taken to avoid catching chicken pox and other contagious illnesses. Hand washing is a simple and easy way to keep germs from entering the body. Always wash hands after using the bathroom, before eating or preparing food, and after coughing or sneezing. This will also help prevent passing on any germs to other people. It is also a good idea to wash hands after being in a public place or using public transportation. The chicken pox virus cannot survive for very long outside a human body, but it can live for a few hours on a doorknob, railing, or telephone—just long enough to be picked up by another person. People should try to avoid rubbing their eyes or touching their nose or mouth without washing hands first. About fifteen to twenty seconds of scrubbing with

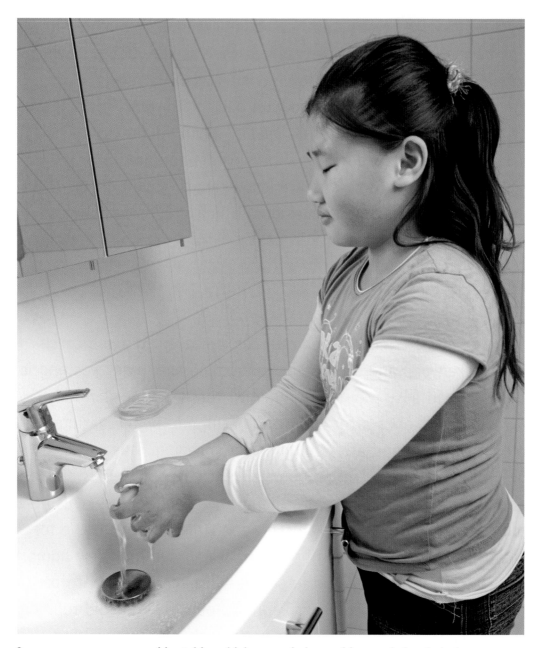

One way a person can avoid catching chicken pox is by washing one's hands to keep germs from entering the body.

warm water and soap should do the trick. Or if no sink is available, there are convenient alcohol-based wipes that also kill the germs on hands.

DIAGNOSING CHICKEN POX

There is usually not much that needs to be done to diagnose chicken pox. A health care professional can usually identify the infection just from the itchy, bumpy rash. If there is any concern that the illness may be a more serious disease, such as smallpox, there are tests that can be done to confirm that it is really just varicella. Doctors can take a sample of the fluid from within one of the bumps and test it using antibodies against the virus made in a laboratory. If the antibodies stick to the virus, then the test is positive for varicella. This type of test only

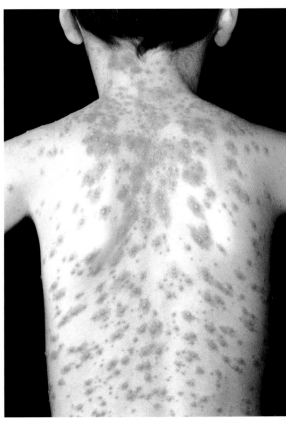

Diagnosing chicken pox is usually very easy, as the telltale blisters are a sure sign of the virus.

takes a few hours to return a result. There are also other laboratory tests that can confirm the varicella virus is responsible for an infection, but some take several days and are rarely used.

TREATMENT

For otherwise healthy children, chicken pox does not require any special medication or treatment. Getting plenty of rest can help beat the infection. If chicken pox sores develop in the mouth, eating only soft, bland foods can be helpful because spicy, acidic, or crunchy foods can be painful to eat.

Even though the rash may be very itchy and uncomfortable, people with chicken pox must try to stop themselves from scratching the sores and scabs. Scratching slows down the healing process and can lead to infections and cause permanent scars on the skin. It is impossible to completely prevent someone from scratching the chicken pox rash, so fingernails should also be kept short and clean in order to prevent secondary skin infection. People who find it difficult to stop scratching may try putting gloves on their hands, especially

One way to help ease the itchy feeling from chickenpox is to apply calamine lotion to the affected area.

at night. If the itching is particularly severe, a doctor can prescribe medication such as an antihistamine, to help stop the itching.

A doctor may allow the use of a lotion or cream applied to the skin to control the itching. Calamine lotion works well for chicken pox, just as it does for insect bites and poison ivy. Taking a cool bath can also calm itchy skin. Daily baths will help keep the skin clean and decrease the chance of developing a skin infection in addition to the chicken pox rash. For added itch relief, sprinkle the bath water with baking soda, uncooked oatmeal, or a special kind of oatmeal that easily dissolves called colloidal oatmeal.

Acetaminophen and ibuprofen are two drugs that can be used to treat a mild fever. Aspirin should never be used to treat a fever or headache associated with chicken pox. In fact, aspirin should not be given to adults or children to treat symptoms of any viral infection because of the small risk of developing a condition called Reye's syndrome. Although rare, people with a viral illness who take aspirin are at risk for developing this severe disease that can cause liver failure, swelling in the brain, and even death.

Medications specifically made to treat viruses may be recommended for people who are at increased risk for developing serious complications. The antiviral drug acyclovir is only available by a doctor's prescription and may lessen

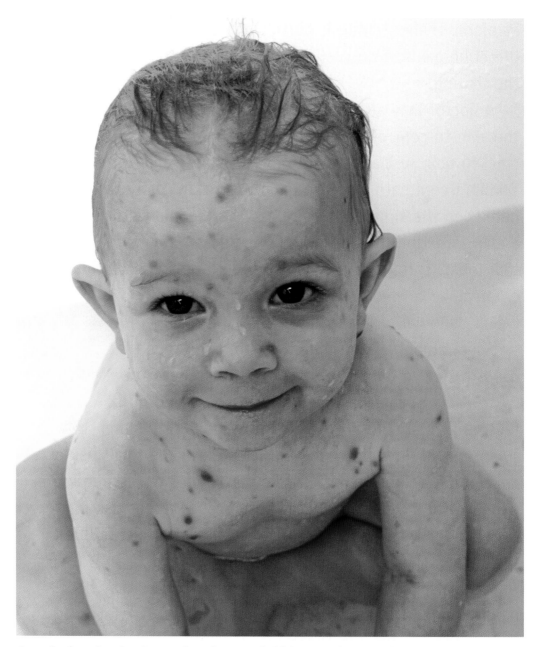

Over the last decade, the number of cases of chicken pox has steadily declined because of the vaccine.

the symptoms and shorten the duration of the chicken pox infection.

Chicken pox was, until the past decade, a disease that nearly everyone had during childhood. Now, with the development of an effective vaccine, the number of cases of chicken pox continues to decline each year. If all children today were to be vaccinated, it is possible that chicken pox could be eliminated just like smallpox and other infectious diseases throughout history. Fewer childhood cases of chicken pox also means a decrease in the number of people who develop shingles later in life. Perhaps someday chicken pox will be an illness that children only read about in books like this one.

GLOSSARY

antibodies—The proteins produced by cells in response to a foreign substance.

antigens—The substances present on a pathogen that allow the immune system to recognize it as a foreign invader.

bone marrow—The soft tissue inside bones, which contains many blood vessels and produces red and white blood cells.

clinical trials—Planned experiments to evaluate the effectiveness and safety of medications, vaccines, or medical devices by testing their effects on volunteer participants.

complications—Diseases or conditions that develop during the course of or as a result of another disease or illness.

contagious—Easily passed on between individuals.

DNA—Abbreviation for deoxyribonucleic acid; a molecule that holds the genetic information that is passed along to the next generation.

genes—Tiny parts of cells that determine specific traits and provide instructions for making every protein needed for life. Genes are made from DNA or RNA.

host—The human, animal, or plant that a fungus or virus lives in or on to survive.

immune system—The system that protects the body from foreign substances, cells, and infection by recognizing these foreign invaders and destroying them.

immunity—The ability to resist a disease.

immunization—A treatment that uses a vaccine to prevent the development of a specific infection.

infectious—Able to spread infection.

inflammation—The swelling of tissues due to infection or injury.

lymphocytes—White blood cells that are either B-cells or T-cells.

microbe—A microorganism or germ.

microorganisms—Tiny organisms of microscopic or less than microscopic size.

molecules—Small units of an organism or object involved in chemical reactions.

pathogen—Bacteria, fungi, viruses, or other substances that can cause disease.

proteins—The complex substances found in cells that are necessary to carry out essential life functions.

replicating—The process of making copies of a virus using the cells and proteins of the host.

RNA—Abbreviation of ribonucleic acid; a molecule that contains genes and is associated with the control of all cellular activities.

susceptible—Having little resistance to a specific infectious disease and capable of being infected.

symptoms—Physical conditions that indicate the presence of a disease or other disorder.

thymus—An organ located in the center of the upper chest where T-cells grow and mature.

torso—The main part of the human body apart from the head, arms, and legs.

vaccine—A preparation of killed, weakened, or fully infectious microbes that is given (often by injection) to provide protection from a particular disease.

virus—A particle able to multiply and cause disease within an organism.

FIND OUT MORE

Book
Weitzman, Elizabeth. *Let's Talk About Having Chicken Pox*. New
York, NY: Rosen Publishing Group, 2003.

Web Sites
**BAM! Body and Mind—Centers for Disease Control and
Prevention (CDC)**
http://www.bam.gov

KidsHealth for Kids
http://www.kidshealth.org/

**National Institute of Environmental Health Sciences
(NIEHS) Kids' Pages: You and Your Genes**
http://kids.niehs.nih.gov/genes/home.htm

INDEX

Page numbers for illustrations are in **boldface**

ABOUT THE AUTHOR

Gretchen Hoffmann, MS, enjoys learning and writing about many topics in health and science. She has research experience in molecular biology and virology from her work at the Boyce Thompson Institute in Ithaca, NY, and holds degrees in Biological Sciences from Cornell University and in Biomedical Journalism from New York University. She currently works in medical communications, where her expertise spans a wide range of therapeutic areas, including infectious disease, nephrology, gastroenterology, cardiology, immunology, and diabetes. In addition to *Chicken Pox*, Ms. Hoffmann is the author of three other Health Alert titles and has also been published in Scholastic's classroom magazine, *Science World*. She lives in Valhalla, New York, with her husband, Bill, and their dog, Rudy.